Dump Dinners
By
Cathy Mitchell

ISBN: 978-0-9895865-4-2
Printed and bound in the United States of America

10 9 8 7 6 5 4 3

Telebrands Press
79 Two Bridges Road
Fairfield, NJ 07004
www.telebrands.com

About the Author

Cathy has been cooking for 60 years, starting at her Grandmother's side, standing on a stool.

She never refers to herself as a chef, but rather a great home cook who enjoys making simple, easy meals with ordinary ingredients. She has been sharing those ideas on television since her first commercial in 1989, introducing America to the electric sandwich maker, and in typical Cathy fashion, making a lot more than sandwiches.

Her kitchen has always been the gathering place for friends and family and she loves to share her recipes and cooking hints while she prepares meals or snacks, often testing out new recipes on a willing group of "Tasters".

She has an extended family of 5 adult children, ranging in age from 31 to 43, and 10 grandkids from 1 to 20. One of her favorite stories is overhearing her oldest son's response, when a dinner guest commented before dinner that he didn't really like something on the menu. He said, "Well maybe not before, but you haven't tried my Mom's yet!"

Foreword

DUMP dinners have been around for as long as cooks have been looking for fast and easy ways to create a meal. Though a somewhat unflattering name, the results are nothing short of delicious, and in most cases, nutritious, too! It is difficult to find dinner recipes that are easier to make than dump dinners, and with the exception of prepping the ingredients, you really have very little to do to assemble it. These recipes are great for beginning cooks, especially young ones, as even small children can enjoy making dinner for the entire family with a few simple ingredients.

SINCE time is always of the essence these days, the dump dinner gang want to make it even easier by offering do-ahead tips and variations. With the growing awareness of good nutrition, most of the recipes have calorie counts as well as use fresh fruits and vegetables, less fat in cooking, and focus on lean meats for preparation.

IN order to strike that healthy balance between nutrition and satisfaction, variety is key. These recipes offer a great deal of variety while helping the everyday cook to expand their repertoire, while supplying the body with all of the nutrients it requires. The current USDA food Guide Pyramid state that eating a wide variety of foods in amounts appropriate for healthy weight is perhaps the single most key to living a healthy lifestyle and avoiding serious health risks.

THIS cookbook is proof that you don't have to sacrifice taste upon the throne of nutrition or health. So serve up a healthy portion of dump dinners for fast, easy, satisfying meals for a fraction of the cost, and in half the time. ENJOY!

Table of Contents

BEEF

Baked Porcupine Meatballs

A little more work but so worth it...let the kids roll the meatballs

Ingredients:
1 1/2 pound lean ground beef
2/3 cup long-grain rice, uncooked
1/2 cup water
½ envelope Lipton onion soup mix (1 heaping tablespoon)
or 1/4 cup finely chopped onion
1 teaspoon seasoned salt
1/4 teaspoon garlic powder
1/8 teaspoon pepper

Topping
1 large can (15 ounces) tomato sauce
1 cup water
2 teaspoons Worcestershire sauce

Directions:
1. Mix ground beef with rice, 1/2 cup of water, chopped onion, seasoned salt, garlic powder, and pepper. Save dishes and do this in the pan.
2. Shape porcupine ground beef mixture by tablespoon into 1 1/2-inch balls, and place into ungreased 9 x 13 baking dish. You can also press mixture into bottom of pan and using a spatula, separate into squares, leaving about ½ inch between the rows. Meat squares taste the same as meatballs but don't roll off the plate as easily.
3. Mix the remaining ingredients and pour over the porcupine meatballs.
4. Cover and bake at 350° F. in oven for about 45 minutes. Uncover and bake porcupine meatballs 15 to 20 minutes longer. Serves 4 to 6.

Beefy Biscuit Bake

Ingredients:
1 ½ pounds cooked ground beef (see easy make ahead
BROWNED GROUND BEEF recipe)
½ envelope Lipton Onion Soup mix (about 1 heaping Tablespoon)
1 8 oz package cream cheese, softened
1 can Cream of Mushroom soup
¼ cup milk
¼ cup sliced ripe olives (optional)
1 small can mushrooms, drained (optional)
½ teaspoon seasoned salt
¼ teaspoon pepper
1 7 oz can biscuits
Melted butter
Parmesan cheese

Directions:
1. Preheat oven to 375 degrees F.
2. Spray a 2 quart casserole dish with nonstick spray.
3. Mix soup, cream cheese, milk, onion soup mix, salt and
   pepper in casserole until smooth.
4. Add ground beef, olives and/or mushrooms and stir to blend.
5. Bake for 30 minutes until hot and bubbly.
6. Arrange biscuits on top, return to oven and bake 10 to 15 minutes
   until biscuits are browned. Brush biscuits with melted butter
   and sprinkle lightly with parmesan cheese if desired.
   Serves 4 to 6

HINT: *Add a 16 oz package frozen vegetable like peas and carrots to
meat mixture before baking if desired.*

Easiest Meatloaf Ever

Ingredients:
1 ½ pounds ground meat, beef or turkey or mixture of 2
1 cup water
1 egg
1 box Stove Top Stuffing Mix (unprepared)

Directions:
1. Preheat oven to 350 degrees F.
2. Spray 9 x 13 baking pan with nonstick spray.
3. Break meat apart into chunks and drop in pan. Add egg to water and blend with a fork.
4. Add stuffing mix and egg water to pan, blend together with hands or large fork or spatula. (As my granddaughter says, "smoosh" it together).
5. After mixing, form into a loaf in the center of pan. Bake for 45 minutes.

Easy Oven Cheeseburger Sliders

No frying, no guessing, cut these burgers to size AFTER they cook!

Ingredients:
1 ½ pounds lean ground beef
¼ cup bread or cracker crumbs
½ package Lipton Onion Soup mix (about 1 heaping tablespoon)
3-4 slices cheese
1 package (12 count)Kings Hawaiian Dinner Rolls, or slider buns

Directions:
1. Preheat oven to 400 degrees F.
2. Place beef, crumbs and soup mix in 9 x 13 pan, then mix together and press into single layer covering the bottom of pan.
3. Use a fork to poke holes thru meat.
4. Bake for 30 minutes. Meat will shrink away from the sides of the pan.
5. Hold meat in place with a spatula, drain away liquid into disposable container, then cover with layer of cheese and return to oven until cheese is melted.
6. Remove from oven and cut into 12 squares.
7. Place on buns and serve with desired toppings such as lettuce, tomato, pickle, etc. Makes 12 sliders.

CHICKEN

Chicken and Mini Dumplings

Ingredients:
4 Boneless, skinless chicken breasts
1 can Cream of Chicken soup
1 Small Onion, chopped
¾ cup celery, chopped (about 3 ribs)
1 egg
½ teaspoon poultry seasoning
½ teaspoon salt
¼ teaspoon pepper
1 tube refrigerator biscuits (7 ounce)

Directions:
1. Preheat oven to 350 degrees F.
2. Place chicken pieces (I like to cut them in half) in a 9 by 13 pan sprayed with nonstick spray.
3. In a bowl, combine soup, celery, onion, egg and seasonings. Mix until blended.
4. Cut each biscuit into 8 or 10 small pieces, then add to bowl and stir gently.
5. Pour sauce evenly over chicken.
6. Bake for about 1 hour, until chicken is done and biscuit pieces have puffed and browned.
   Serves 4

Easy Peasy Chicken and Rice

Ingredients:
4 boneless, skinless chicken breasts, cut in quarters
2 cups frozen peas
1 cup uncooked white rice (not instant)
1 can cream soup, chicken, mushroom, celery (Your choice)
1 envelope Lipton onion soup mix
2 cups hot water

Directions:
1. Preheat oven to 375 degrees F.
2. Nonstick spray a 2 quart casserole dish with a lid.
3. Put rice, both soups, water, and peas in casserole and blend with spoon or whisk.
4. Add chicken pieces and stir together.
5. Cover and bake 1 hour until rice has absorbed water and chicken is cooked through.
   Serves 4

Oh So Easy Chicken Dinner

Ingredients:
4-6 boneless, skinless chicken breasts
1-2 cans green beans,
2-3 potatoes, cubed
1 packet Good Seasons Italian Dressing Mix
1 stick butter, melted with 1 teaspoon Lawry's Seasoned Salt

Directions:
1. Spray a 9" x 13" dish with cooking spray.
2. Empty one or two cans of drained green beans down one side of the baking dish
3. Place chicken breasts in the middle of the dish in a line
4. Put cut potatoes on the third side of the dish.
5. Drizzle melted butter over the top of everything.
6. Sprinkle dry Italian Dressing Mix over the entire dish.
7. Cover with foil and bake at 350 degrees for one hour, removing foil for last 15 minutes
8. Remove from oven, and serve.
   Serves 4 to 6

MEXICAN

Baked Chicken Fajitas

Ingredients:

1 pound boneless, skinless chicken breasts, cut into strips

1 (15 oz) can diced tomatoes

1 (4 oz) can diced green chilies

1 medium onion, cut in thin strips

1 large bell pepper, or 1 small green and 1 small red pepper, seeded and cut in thin strips

2 Tablespoons vegetable oil

1 package fajita seasoning mix OR

2 teaspoons chili powder

2 teaspoons cumin

1/2 teaspoon garlic powder

1/2 teaspoon dried oregano

1/4 t. salt

12 flour tortillas, warmed to serve

Directions:

1. Preheat the oven to 400 degrees.

2. Grease a 13×9 baking dish.

3. Mix together chicken, tomatoes, chilies, peppers, and onions in the dish.

4. In a small bowl combine the oil and Fajita Mix OR spices.

5. Drizzle the spice mixture over the chicken and toss to coat.

6. Bake uncovered for 20-25 minutes or until chicken is cooked through and the vegetables are tender.

7. Serve with warmed tortillas. Offer sour cream, guacamole and shredded cheese for garnish.
   Serves 4

Beef and Bean Enchilada Casserole

Ingredients:
1 pound cooked ground beef
(See make ahead browned ground beef recipe)
1 Tablespoon dried minced onion
One 15-ounce can pinto beans, drained
(I use Bush seasoned recipe beans)
One 4-ounce can diced green chilies
1 cup sour cream, mixed with 2 tablespoons flour and
¼ teaspoon garlic powder
Eight 6-inch corn tortillas
1 1/2 cups enchilada sauce
1 1/2 to 2 cups mixed Cheddar- Jack cheese

Directions:
1. Preheat the oven to 350 degrees F. Spray a 2-quart baking dish
   with nonstick spray.
2. Mix meat, onion, beans and chilies together
3. Place half of the tortillas in the bottom of the prepared dish, tearing them apart as needed to cover the bottom (overlapping is fine). Top with half of the meat mixture, spoon half of the sour cream mixture on top of the meat, and drizzle 3/4 cup of the enchilada sauce on top of that. Repeat the layers one more time.
4. Cover with foil and bake for 40 minutes. Uncover, sprinkle with cheese and bake an additional 5 minutes or until the cheese bubbly and melted. Serves 4 to 6

Tips: *Serve with garnishes of choice; Sour cream, guacamole, salsa, chopped tomato, etc.*

Chili Mac
Short name...Long on Flavor!

Ingredients:
1 pound lean ground beef
3 cups hot water
1 can (15 oz) tomato sauce
1 envelope chili seasoning (I only use Chili-O by French's)
1 box, 16 ounces, rotini or elbow macaroni
Velveeta slices

Directions:
1. In a large deep skillet or Dutch oven with a cover, place ground beef, tomato sauce, chili seasoning and water. Bring to a boil, stirring a little to break up the hamburger.
2. Once water is boiling, add uncooked pasta, stir, cover and reduce heat. Let simmer about 15 minutes, until water is absorbed by pasta, stirring to mix.
3. Remove from heat, completely cover top with sliced Velveeta, then cover and allow to stand until cheese is well melted.

Note: *This has been a family favorite for over 40 years. According to everyone who has ever eaten this, it MUST be served with buttered corn kernels. Never add the corn to the recipe...I tried once and nobody would eat it!*

So...put a 1 pound bag of frozen corn in a covered pan with 1/3 cup water, salt and pepper and 2 tablespoons butter. Cover and cook about 10 minutes, just until water is gone and only the butter is left. Do not drain. At my house the spoonful of corn must go on top of the mac! Nobody spoiled at my house!

Chili Dog Casserole

Ingredients:
2 cans (15 oz. each) chili with beans
8 hot dogs
8 flour tortillas (6 inch)
½ cup Shredded Mild Cheddar Cheese

Directions:
1. Heat oven to 400°F.
2. Spread chili into bottom of 11 x 7 inch baking dish.
3. Place 1 hot dog on each tortilla; roll up. Place, seam-sides down, over chili.
4. Spray lightly with nonstick spray to aid in browning tortilla.
5. Bake 15 min. or until hot dogs are heated through and tortilla is browned.
6. Sprinkle with cheese and bake until cheese is melted, about 5 more minutes.

Doritos Cheesy Chicken

Ingredients:
2 cups precooked chicken, chopped (see make ahead
chicken recipe) or 2 cans chicken breast (like Swanson's) drained.
1 cup sour cream
1 can cream of chicken soup
1 can Rotel tomatoes or 1 ½ cups chunky salsa
1 can corn, drained
2 cups shredded cheese, like Colby Jack or Mexican, divided
1 bag Nacho Cheese Doritos, coarsely crushed or any
leftover tortilla chips (4 to 5 cups or more)

Directions:
1. Preheat oven to 350 degrees F.
2. Spray 9 x 13 pan with nonstick spray
3. Cover bottom of pan with 1/2 of the crushed chips (I often use
plain chips here and save Doritos for the top)
4. Dump all other ingredients in a bowl, saving half the cheese.
5. Mix together and pour over chips
6. Top with remaining chips and bake for 20 to 25 minutes until hot
7. Sprinkle remaining cheese over the top and return to oven
   until melted
I serve with 1 package prepared Spanish rice, Like Knorr Fiesta Sides
My family likes to fill warm flour tortillas with the chicken!

Oven Tacos

Ingredients:

1 ½ cups precooked ground beef
(see easy make ahead browned ground beef recipe)
1 can refried beans
1 package taco seasoning
12 prepared taco shells
1 cup shredded cheese

Directions:

1. Preheat oven to 350 degrees F.
2. Mix together beef, beans and seasoning.
3. Divide mixture between 12 shells, filling and standing up in 9 x 13 pan.
4. Sprinkle cheese over tacos, making sure it gets inside each taco.
5. Bake for 15 to 20 minutes until filling is heated thru and cheese is melted.
6. Serve with Shredded lettuce, tomato, olives, sour cream, guacamole or other desired toppings.
   Serves 4 to 6

ITALIAN

Best Baked Ravioli

Ingredients:
1 bag (25 Oz. Bag) Frozen Ravioli, your choice of meat, cheese, or veggie
1 jar (26 Oz. Jar) Marinara Sauce
2 cups Shredded Mozzarella Cheese
2 cups fresh baby spinach
Parmesan Cheese

Directions:
1. Preheat oven to 400°F.
2. Spray bottom and sides of a 9×13 rectangular baking dish with cooking spray.
3. Spread 3/4 cup of the pasta sauce in baking dish. Arrange half of the frozen ravioli in a single layer over the sauce; top with half of the remaining pasta sauce and half of the mozzarella cheese.
5. Spread spinach over cheese and repeat layer, starting with ravioli, remainder of sauce, and rest of cheese. Sprinkle with Parmesan cheese.
6. Cover with aluminum foil and bake for 30 minutes. Remove foil; bake uncovered for 10 to 15 minutes longer or until bubbly and hot in the center. Let stand for 10 minutes before serving.
Serves 4 to 6

Deeply D'Lish Pizza

Ingredients:
1 tube Grands biscuits
1 cup marinara sauce (I use Prego)
Pepperoni slices (I used Hormel Turkey Pepperoni)
Sliced olives
1 cup mozzarella cheese shredded

Directions:
1. Cut each biscuit into 6 pieces and drop in bottom of glass or ceramic baking pan sprayed with nonstick spray.
2. Cut pepperoni slices into quarters and distribute over biscuits. Add sliced olives and then a light layer of sauce, about 1 cup. (Add in blops, and do not cover entire surface)
3. Sprinkle with light layer of cheese.
4. Bake at 350 25 to 30 minutes.

HINT: You can use any toppings as long as they will cook properly in 25 minutes. Avoid raw meat.

Skillet Pasta & Beef Dinner

Ingredients:
1 pound lean ground beef
One 24 ounce jar pasta sauce
2 cups hot water
2 cups uncooked rotini pasta
1 cup shredded mozzarella cheese (about 4 oz.)
1 teaspoon seasoned salt
½ teaspoon garlic powder

Directions:
1. Place ground beef in a large skillet with a cover.
2. Add 2 cups of hot water and jar of pasta sauce and salt and garlic powder.
3. Bring to a boil over high heat, stirring to break up ground beef.
4. Stir in uncooked rotini, reduce heat to medium and cook covered, stirring occasionally, 15 minutes or until rotini is tender.
5. Remove from heat, sprinkle with cheese. Cover and let stand until cheese is melted.
   Serves 4

OTHER

Easy Smothered Pork Chops

Ingredients:
4 regular cut bone-in pork chops
1 can cream of mushroom soup
1 cup uncooked rice, (not instant)
2 cups hot water
One 16 oz bag frozen peas
1 envelope Lipton Onion Soup Mix

Directions:
1. Preheat oven to 375 degrees F.
2. Spray 9 x 13 pan with nonstick spray.
3. Dump mushroom soup, rice, and hot water into pan and stir together until well mixed.
5. Stir in peas.
6. Place pork chops on top, pressing down into rice mixture.
7. Sprinkle envelope of dry soup mix evenly over all.
8. Bake 1 hour until chops are done and rice has absorbed liquid.
   Serves 4

Easy Cheesy Breakfast Bake

Ingredients:
1 tube Grands biscuits, separated and cut in quarters.

1 cup egg beaters or 3 eggs beaten with ¼ cup milk.

1 cup precooked sausage crumbles or 8 slices precooked bacon, cut into 1" pieces.

¾ cup shredded cheese

Directions:
1. Preheat oven to 350
2. Spray 9 x 13 pan with nonstick spray
3. Arrange biscuit pieces in single layer in pan
4. Distribute bacon or sausage evenly over biscuits
5. Pour egg over all
6. Sprinkle evenly with cheese.
7. Bake for 20 to 25 minutes, until egg is set and biscuits are brown.
   Serves 4 to 6

Tater-Tot Casserole

Ingredients:

1 pound browned, ground beef

1/2 envelope Lipton onion soup mix
(about 1 heaping tablespoon)

1 (10 1/2 ounce) can condensed cream of celery
or cream of chicken soup (undiluted)

1 16 oz package frozen tater tots

1 cup shredded cheddar cheese

Directions:

1. Preheat oven to 375 degrees.
2. In a casserole dish, combine cooked ground beef & dry
   onion soup mix, and cream soup.
3. Top mixture with tater tots.
4. Bake, uncovered, for 30-40 minutes till bubbly and tots are
   golden brown.
5. Remove from oven & top with cheese, return to oven until melted.
   Serves 4

MAKE AHEAD

Easy Make Ahead Browned Ground Beef

When you come home from the store with ground beef, buy 4 or 5 pounds and then put it in a large deep pan, cover with water and cook over a medium heat, stirring occasionally until meat has no pink color.

Drain in a large colander, divide, and then transfer to plastic storage bags or containers. You can freeze or refrigerate until ready to use.

Hint: *If you cooked 5 pounds divide into 5 bags so you have 1 pound servings = to recipe calling for 1 pound ground beef, cooked and drained. If you store in a large container, 2 loosely packed cups = about 1 pound. 6 pounds cooked will = 4 bags of 1 ½ pounds for recipe calling for 1 ½ pounds cooked and drained ground beef, or about 3 loosely packed cups.*

This will work for all dump recipes calling for ground beef and eliminate the extra step of stovetop browning.

Easy Make Ahead Shredded Chicken

When on sale, buy boneless, skinless chicken breasts. Put in a large deep pan, cover with water and simmer until chicken has no pink inside (about 30 to 45 minutes). Remove from water, allow to cool, then shred or cube, and pack in plastic bags. I use one sandwich bag for each breast piece cooked. 1 bag = 1cup shredded or chopped, cooked chicken.